KENNETH TURNER

DRIED FLOWERS

KENNETH TURNER

DRIED FLOWERS

TEXT BY SALLY GRIFFITHS

PHOTOGRAPHS BY ANDREW TWORT

additional arrangements by Simon Brown

WEIDENFELD & NICOLSON

LONDON

CONTENTS

INTRODUCTION
Terracotta gallery

In a carefree moment, I christened this setting "my growing fireplace". This descriptive line stuck and I can now see why. Terracotta pots are of a rare and exotic colour and, although they are a major element in the garden,

nobody, as far as I know, has constructed a terracotta platform for floral display. I promise the task is far less awesome and onerous than you might think.

GARDEN FLOWERS
Blue and white charm

*Dried flowers allow you to bring the garden
indoors for year-round pleasure. I favour
glorious massed bunches and, depending on the mood,
will opt for single flower arrangements or extravagant
combinations of colours and textures. There is no limit to
the kind of container which can be used – traditional vases,
old boxes, antique urns – it's time to let your
imagination run riot.*

ABOVE AND
LEFT
*Dried lavender is
deservedly an all-
time favourite. It
is easy to dry and
retains its scent,
reminiscent of the*
*English summer
or sun-baked
fields in Provence.
It looks equally
good in small
bouquets or large
bunches, set off
with classical urns.*

11

Floral fusions

We all cherish blue and white china, so gorgeously simple and decorative and, amongst all glazed surfaces, possessing that rarest of qualities: the gift of enhancing floral company. Here is one of many such assemblies made for my own home: larkspur, rambling roses, peonies, lavenders and hydrangeas. I confess that the temptation to create what I term these floral fusions is an irresistible daily indulgence.

RIGHT
Although this assembly demands a large quantity of flowers, it is perfect for showing off your garden's harvest. Keep the flowers in groups for this display, as solid blocks of colour create impact.

RIGHT
*An explosion of
colours: dried
zinnias,
hydrangeas,
varieties of seed
pods, eucalyptus
foliage and roses,
plus red
helichrysums in
the foreground.*

ABOVE
*A mass of colour,
from sunshine
yellow through
vibrant orange to
fiery red.*

I sometimes think that there is very little difference between an artist with his palette and blank canvas and myself with my flowers and empty containers. The flowers are my paint; grouped bunches of blooms are my brushstrokes. And, as with the artist and his landscape, I see movement within the tones which I term "pockets" of colour. The components of this floral masterpiece include hydrangeas, Chinese lanterns, larkspur, roses, love-lies-bleeding, alchemilla, echinops, celosia, helichrysum and artichokes. Quite a palette!

ABOVE
In a wicker basket sitting atop an urn, a riot of colour in the form of dried zinnias, Chinese lanterns, achillea, hydrangeas, love-lies-bleeding, seed pods, roses and masses of pink helichrysums.

BELOW
Floral glory in Victorian terracotta: poppy heads, hydrangeas, herbs and nigella set within a collar of wheat and rope, decorated with a posy of poppy heads.

16

ROSES
An eternal classic

Who could not love roses – from the romance of the single red rose to the glory of a summer rose garden in full bloom, from the neat elegance of a tight bud to the sumptuous flamboyance of the full-blown rose. Truly a flower to be celebrated, whether making a solo appearance or forming a partnership with other blooms.

LEFT
*The romance of
the garden –
wine, summer
roses and
candlelight.
Who could ask
for more?*

A truly romantic and aromatic garden party setting, with candlesticks and containers made from cinnamon sticks, preserved greenery and apricot roses. The container (a plastic bowl with cinnamon sticks glued to the exterior) is filled with yet more cinnamon sticks tied into bundles, nuts, dried oranges, clove balls, preserved ivy berries, leaves and spices, plus the delicate dried flowers. The candlesticks were made in the same way, and topped with a circlet of dried roses.

In one way or another, Eros operates in every garden

Michael Pollan   21

Napkin rings seem to act as a contemplative challenge to me. Why not try something quite new and novel I ask myself? I've tried cinnamon sticks, but these pictures show something quite different: a napkin ring created by covering a large curtain ring with preserved greenery and a single rose. Happily, all my dinner guests were wholly approving. What shall I try next?

Flowers always make people better, happier, more helpful; they are sunshine, food and medicine to the soul

Luther Burbank

RIGHT
A mass of rose heads, all carefully picked and dried just at the point of breaking into bloom. Attached to spheres of florists' foam and settled into in a variety of containers, they create a truly arresting display.

My roses are my jewels, the sun and moon my clocks, fruit and water my food and drink

Hester Lucy Stanhope

LEFT
A glass cylinder filled with pot-pourri topped by a semi-sphere of soft orange preserved roses. Perfect for bedrooms.

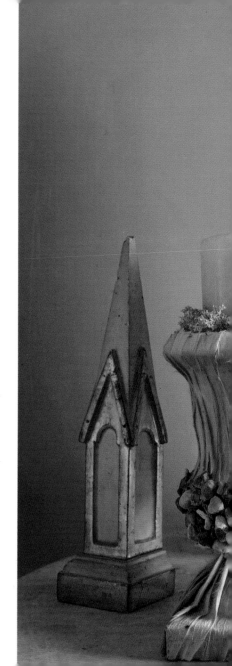

Here are roses preserved in such a way that they retain their texture and colour. They even remain so naturally soft to the touch that most people think they are real. The group of all-white objects on the white marble adds to the unusual delights of the one-colour display. The mound of white roses is surrounded by a ring of lemons with a base of bright foliage in a simple silver container – such a touch of glitter works well in an all-white theme.

RIGHT
A floral display enhanced by antiques. The urn is covered with leaves which have been painted white and decorated with moss, seed pods and pebbles.

26

Red rose, proud rose, sad rose of all my days!
Come near me while I sing the ancient ways

W.B. Yeats

LEFT
*An unusual
silver candle-
basket complete
with pockets:
the perfect foil
for the richness
of red roses.*

RIGHT
*A sweetly scented
pot-pourri of
dried and
preserved roses
displayed within
an antique Scottish
wooden bowl.*

29

LEFT
*Staffordshire
ceramics –
innocent infant
heads and a
pompus grandee
plus grouped
roses, peonies and
lavender. A perfect
decorative theme
for a bedroom.*

31

FOLIAGE
Everlasting elegance

Architectural themes recur in many of my arrangements, especially those designed to be displayed for many a year. Foliage offers many possibilities – the shapes and textures are more structured than those of flowers – and it makes for a visually exciting change of pace. Soft, muted colours, classic containers and a sense of restraint (just a touch) combine to provide an elegance that will stand the test of time in settings both modern and traditional.

ABOVE
Terracotta pot with a slightly unruly head of pine cones.

Here, once again, is a favourite small terracotta pot, complete with a length of birch, structured with wire netting for the reception of your sphere of moss. And which moss to use? Well, take your pick from reindeer moss, lichen moss or bun moss. Place in the company of other treasured objects of varying shape and ancestry for a beautiful and unique still-life decoration.

LEFT
Such a terracotta pot holds its own with the most desirable of objets d'art.

RIGHT
*Another tripartite
group: wheat-
filled containers
stand to attention,
proudly flanking
a terracotta pot of
topiary.*

ABOVE
*A sheaf composed
of preserved
eucalyptus held
within a tie of
rushes or snake
grass, and knotted
with garden rope.*

36

LEFT
*Design for a
pilaster of dried
and preserved
leaves: ideal for a
landing or
dining-room,
indoors or out.*

*These are what I term my "tapestry" designs. If
you can't afford a rare authentic antique tapestry,
why not evolve one to your own design from
preserved leaves? One design was inspired by an
eighteenth-century painting, the other by the border
of a mosaic floor. I especially like the frame of
preserved magnolia leaves which is very effective set
against a natural background of stone or wood.*

RIGHT
*Rural scene in
moss, wheat and
eucalyptus
enframed by
magnolia leaves.
Perfect set against
weathered stone
or timber.*

RIGHT
*One of the charms
of these mock-
topiary decorations
is the opportunity
to vary the
dimensions.*

MOCK
TOPIARY

*A delightful essay in beauty, simplicity – and
rosemary. Select some small plastic pots, embellish
the sides with glued-on rosemary twigs, then shape
wire netting into a basic sphere. Cover this with a
neat head of rosemary to complete the decoration
and trim off any wayward sprigs. They can be
poised atop rosemary stems as supporting trunks.
I think these are rather chic: especially when
displayed in pairs or trios on a dining table or
mantlepiece with candle-lit accompaniment.*

Of the possibilities of visual pleasure to be derived from dried leaves there is no end. Two beguiling girlfriends were off to a supper party and wanted to make their mark on entry. I suggested using a couple of old-fashioned but rather charming clutch handbags in a new way: covering one with preserved leaves and the other with dried dahlias.

LEFT
Formula for a light-hearted touch of magic: cover an old teapot with glued-on leaves. Add flowers to taste. Fun for a summer tea party in the garden.

Appropriate handles give the bags an even more zestful touch, so I used willow branches, also leaf-covered and stapled to the bags. They – girls and bags – were deservedly the belles of the party.

A personal journal, for recording your private
thoughts and special dreams, deserves a unique
treatment. First covered with a neat patchwork
of preserved leaves in contrasting shades of green,
finishing touches are added with brown leaves,
berries and miniature twigs.

STICKS & STONES
And pebbles & twigs

*Don't ever limit yourself solely to using
dried flowers and foliage – experiment with
all manner of treasures gleaned from garden and woods,
shoreline and vegetable plot. Seek out interesting textures
and unusual colours, then let your imagination run riot
to create unusual figurative and abstract objects. You may
surprise yourself with the results of your
forays out of the flower garden!*

These spheres are man-made: one with tiny shells, another with lichen moss, another with dried laurel leaves glued on to a small glass globe. Set a group of spheres of your own creation in a flat metal or ceramic platter and display on a low coffee table. Few of your guests will be able to resist such a collage of spheres within hands' reach. These pale and restrained tones blend together, but for a touch of colour experiment with a mass of rosebuds, each neatly butted up against its neighbour.

RIGHT
Perfect spheres with tempting, tactile overcoats.

49

Black willow

Twigs of black willow are spectacular to work with. You see them here, set on trunks of silver birch and then potted in terracotta containers and topped with pebbles. The conical shape has been filled with tiny speckled quails' eggs, perfect for an up-to-date Easter gift. A favourite client contends that these twisted shapes in black willow have a surrealistic air. Upon reflection, I might be convinced that some of my arrangements are on the modern side!

RIGHT
The contrast of black willow against brick is ideal.

Valentine's Day and flowers go hand in hand but I decided it was time to break away from tradition.

For the modern romantic, I set a tightly packed heart of vibrant preserved red roses on a cushion of rich green moss in a heart-shaped wicker basket, and enclosed the whole thing beneath a black willow cage. A resounding success, I'm sure you'll agree.

The heart is a small thing but desireth great matters

Francis Quarles

RIGHT
The most esoteric components have their quasi-floral charms. These decorations are smooth, uniformly grey stones from the Welsh mountains. The containers are covered with lichen with the stones glued on.

The stone that is rolling can gather no moss

Thomas Tusser

HOW DOES
YOUR
GARDEN
GROW?

Used in this manner, smooth-surfaced stones in shades ranging from deep blue-grey to warm, creamy coffee become objects of great beauty. Here the obelisks have been paired with two urns of brightly coloured pansies but they would look equally as good on thier own. They are perfect for providing interest to the garden in winter. Striking in the extreme, these pebble-covered obelisks provide focal points whether used indoors or out.

SHELLS
For beautiful mementos

The different shapes, colours and textures of sea shells offer myriad possibilities for arrangements. They can be piled into cylindrical glass vases for a whimsical and enthralling decoration, perfect for a bathroom or even a beach house. Alternatively, keep the display simple with just a few special treasures in a small basket. Don't forget sand, natural sponges and driftwood for a constant reminder of faraway shores.

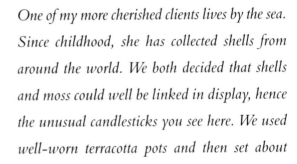

BELOW
An antique potato basket provides the base for a group of mixed shells from distant shores with sea-smoothed driftwood as contrast.

One of my more cherished clients lives by the sea. Since childhood, she has collected shells from around the world. We both decided that shells and moss could well be linked in display, hence the unusual candlesticks you see here. We used well-worn terracotta pots and then set about modelling a mock-spiral eye-stopper. The photograph shows the result: an example of nature's carefree offerings for dramatic display – even on the most modest domestic scale.

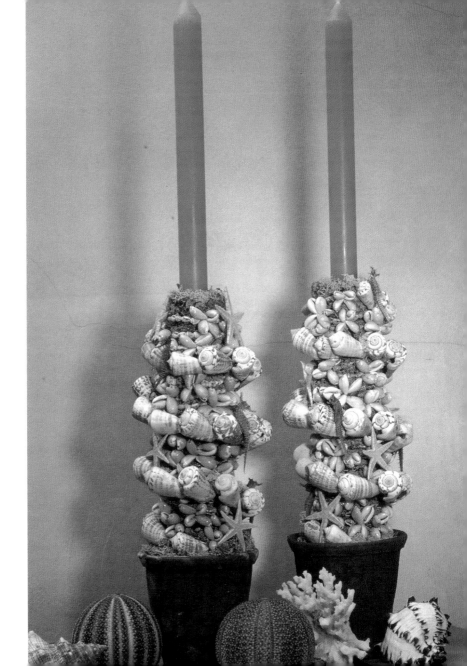

RIGHT
The exotic candlesticks evolved from sea shells and moss plus a few shells scattered around the base.

Here I used a tall, conical rhubarb pot into which I massed wonderful pieces of driftwood picked up on the beaches of Cornwall. I also included large and small shells alongside groups of coral and miniature orchids. It's an easy enough temptation but don't limit yourself to keeping shells in the bathroom – they look equally splendid in a conservatory, hallway or bedroom. A friend took this to heart and set her arrangement atop a small table in her kitchen. To complement the picture, a garniture of old Indian pots filled with pot-pourri and short candles emerging from a bed of moss in old terracotta pots adorn the table. Shell textures, colours and shapes are just as beautiful as those of flowers, or perhaps it's the other way around?

RIGHT
Shells acting as flowers or, possibly, vice-versa. Try your hand at copying this large scale theatrical display.

Text copyright © Kenneth Turner Ltd 1997
Photographs copyright © Andrew Twort 1997
Design and layout copyright © Weidenfeld &
Nicolson 1997

Kenneth Turner has asserted his right to be identified as the
Author of this Work.

First published in 1997 by
George Weidenfeld & Nicolson Limited
The Orion Publishing Group
Orion House
5 Upper St. Martin's Lane
London WC2H 9EA

A CIP catalogue record for this book is available from the
British Library

ISBN 0-297-82348-5

Designed by Lisa Tai
Edited by Gillian Haslam

All photographs by Andrew Twort except:
Top page 2, 16, 41, 60: Marie-Louise Avery;
Page 38-9: Phil Starling
Page 42 Teapot: Simon Wheeler
Page 42-3: Kiloran Howard
Page 59, 62-3: John Miller

All Kenneth Turner products are available from
Kenneth Turner Ltd., 125 Mount St, London W1Y 5HA
Tel: 0171 355 3880   Fax: 0171 495 1607

Printed in Italy

ACKNOWLEDGEMENTS

The author and publishers would
like to thank the following for
providing items for photography:

Nicole Fabre Antique Textiles
592 Kings Road
London SW6
Tel: 0171 384 3112

Guinevere Antiques
578 Kings Road
London SW6
Tel: 0171 736 2917

Myriad Antiques
13 Portland Road
London W11
Tel: 0171 727 7154

O.F. Wilson
Queen's Elm Parade
Old Church Street
London SW3
Tel: 0171 352 9554

David Black
96 Portland Road
London W11
Tel: 0171 727 2566

Alistair Sampson Antiques
120 Mount Street
London W1
Tel: 0171 409 1789

The O'Shea Gallery
120A Mount St.
London W1
Tel: 0171 629 1122

Many thanks also to the Kenneth
Turner team:
Barry, Laura, Karl and
Christopher.